Misdiagnosed in the Church
Copyright © Richard Adkins
ISBN: 978-1-958186-34-3
LOC: ACCEPTED

Publisher, Editor, and Book Design:
Fiery Beacon Publishing House, LLC
Fiery Beacon Consulting and Publishing Group

Graphics: FBPH Graphics Team, Dashona Smith

MISDIAGNOSED

IN THE

CHURCH

BISHOP RICHARD J. ADKINS

Table of Contents

Dedication
Acknowledgements
The Foreword

Chapter 1
Misdiagnosed in the Church   11

Chapter 2
Five-Fold Ministry   13

Chapter 3
Leadership Roles   19

Chapter 4
The Apostolic Mantle   23

Chapter 5
Lay Hands Suddenly On No Man   29

Chapter 6
Unprocessed Ministries   37

Chapter 7
Rebellious Elders   45

Chapter 8
Fruitless Pastors   53

Chapter 9
The Evangelist   63

Chapter 10
He Gave Some Teachers   71

Chapter 11
The Prophet   77

Chapter 12
Where are the Deacons   85

Chapter 13
Dressed for the Wrong Occasion   93

Chapter 14
The Gift of Apostle   101

Chapter 15
The Bishopric   109

Chapter 16
The Bonus Chapter (Vocabulary and Terms)   121

A Dedication   133

Notes   141

Connect with the Author   143

Dedication

I dedicate this book to God, whose perfect plan revealed in scripture gives me peace in this tumultuous world.

To my family, friends and ministry partners...
It is your love, prayers and support that give me the strength and resources to carry out that which God has called me to. Thank you.

To my Spiritual Parents....
My spiritual father in the Lord's Church, Bishop George Bloomer (Bethany Family Worship Center), and my spiritual mother, Apostle Janice Thomas and Pops, Bishop Randall Thomas (His Kingdom Ministries), thank you! Words will never be able to convey my appreciation for you all, your prayers and your pour.

To my Wife of more than a decade, Lady Apostle Shaun Adkins.... Thank you for your prophetic sound that pushed me into writing this book. I will love you forever.

Additional Acknowledgements

First and foremost, I want to thank the Lord for giving His Word. I harbor a deep love for scripture and count it an honor and privilege to have been called by God to both study and teach His biblical truths.

I want to thank Impact/Redzone City of Refuge Church - you guys absolutely rock! I also want to thank F.A.L.I.C., an awesome fellowship and reformation of which I have had the honor of serving as Presiding Prelate for ten years.

I send my deepest appreciation and love to my wife, Lady Apostle Shaun Adkins, my children, grandchildren and godchildren for your love and encouragement.

Thank you Prophet Brandi Rojas and your FYreHouse team for making this book happen.

Finally, thank you to the hundreds and thousands of followers, prayer partners, and ministry supporters. This could not exist without you.

The Foreword

I was introduced to Bishop Richard Adkins in December 2022. Bishop Adkins had been serving in the Ecclesiastical order of Simon of Cyrene, within The United Apostolic and Charismatic Church. I had recently been placed as a the Abbott over the erection of that order within the ecclesiastical diocese of the Middle Eastern states where I was serving as the Episcopal Prelate. At the time of our meeting, it was apparent to me Bishop Adkins had a sincere desire to perfect his bishopric.

Like many clergy, he found himself placed in Episcopal service without the benefit of all of the attributes of preparation and training that is needed to successfully perform their duties. He was determined to learn and grow in his assignment. Bishop Atkins has, in his character, an attribute of being teachable, despite the fact that he had been placed in high office within the church recognized that he desired and needed strengthening. Already having knowledge about many aspects of the polity and practice of the church, Bishop Adkins wanted to know more about the ecclesiology, doctrine, theological underpinnings and overall development of the Episcopacy.

Bishop Atkins proved to be a quick study and one who, even when corrected concerning being overdressed or protocols of walking within Episcopal prelature, and ceremony never resisted or acted pridefully, but instead, accept the correction and quickly adapted.

This book is an expression and biopsy of his journey he is going through. As his diocesan Bishop, we share a synergy and mutual respect that is based upon trusted communications, which within the religious community is very rare. This book will hopefully will help younger clergy who are coming into Episcopal honors to learn how to negotiate the path to preparation before placement by attachment to trusted and knowledgeable authorities. It has been my privilege to impart to him all that has been given to me in over forty years of professional Christian ministry.

I believe that Bishop Adkins has the opportunity to ensure that the future of the church is secured and safe as we passed these vital elements of tradition, preparation and training before placement. This book is designed to do just that.

Vero Quid Muneris,
(In Truth and Service)

The Rt. Rev. Ab. David Jerome Davis, Sr.
Th.B., M.Div., STM, DD, OSSC

Chapter 1
Misdiagnosed in the Church

Misdiagnose: (verb)
"make in incorrect diagnosis."

Being misdiagnosed can cause a dangerous condition to go untreated or result in you receiving treatments you did not even need. What is another word for "misdiagnosis"? Misidentification, mis-judgement and misrecognition are just a few that speak to the reality that such errors can cause physically, emotionally, financially and spiritually. As we prepare for the literary road head, allow me a few moments to share about the various questions that may come to mind.

Why is misdiagnosis bad?

If a person does not receive an accurate diagnosis, they may not receive timely care and their condition can worsen. In addition, if a doctor fails to diagnose a patient's condition, the patient may lose the possibility of survival.

How do we fix a misdiagnosis?

To overcome this, you must first get the correct diagnosis for your issue. Often, this requires getting a second, and sometimes even a third, or fourth opinion. When we do not have anyone to advocate for us, this can cause these extremities be too likely and necessary. Once we are able to get clarity and the answers we need, we can then proceed with the proper treatment plan.

Can a misdiagnosis be traumatic?

Of course, it can. Being diagnosed or misdiagnosed are both traumatic in their own right. One may experience a new wave of emotional trauma as well as potentially lost time from proper treatment.

What is the evidence of a misdiagnosis?

At the onset of a diagnosis, usually a treatment plan, prescriptions and potentially both are presented. If after treatments, your condition does not improve, this may indicate that you have been misdiagnosed.

Chapter 2
Five-Fold Ministry

11 And [His gifts to the church were varied and] He Himself appointed some as apostles [special messengers, representatives], some as prophets [who speak a new message from God to the people], some as evangelists [who spread the good news of salvation], and some as pastors and teachers [to shepherd and guide and instruct],

Ephesians 4:11 (GNT)

11 So Christ himself gave the apostles, the prophets, the evangelists, the pastors and teachers,

Ephesians 4:11 (NIV)

11 And He Himself gave some *to be* apostles, some prophets, some evangelists, and some pastors and teachers,

Ephesians 4:11 (NKJV)

Impatient lay members become unprocessed ministers who turn into rebellious Elders, become fruitless Pastors and eventually illegitimate Bishops. Allow this to sink in for a moment or two. As we look on Facebook and other social media platforms, we are all privy to those upcoming elevations, ordinations, consecrations, affirmations and installations. When someone is elevated in the kingdom, we must first remember that the elevation was not from man, but instead came from God.

> For not from the east, nor from the west,
> Nor from the desert comes exaltation.
> But God is the Judge;
> He puts down one and lifts up another.
>
> Psalm 75:6-7

If we research, we will find that there are fifty or more bible verses in the bible that speak on promotion.

Promotion is a common theme frequently explored in the bible. This goes beyond traditional concepts of career advancement or social elevation; instead focusing on spiritual growth and maturation and the reward that comes with faithfulness and obedience to God's will becomes key. The bible portrays promotion as a divine favor — a reward from God that accompanies living by His principles and precepts.

What Does the Bible Say About Promotion?

The bible contains numerous verses on the theme of promotion. It teaches that promotion is not the results of mankind's efforts but is a blessing bestowed by God. According to these verses, God is the one who lifts up and brings down. God is seen as the ultimate provider of mankind's fortunes. In essence, God is shown as the One who promotes and demotes according to His divine plan and timing.

Why Does God Promote?

According to the Bible, promotion is a reward for the faithfulness, obedience and spiritual maturation. God promotes as a form of discernment; He sees the heart and knows who is ready for more responsibility or greater blessings. God often uses trials, hardships, and tribulations to refine His people before promoting them, teaching them life-changing lessons in the process. He desires to mold us into the image of His son, Jesus Christ. This is often reflected by His decisions to promote or not to promote.

Who Gets Promoted According to the Bible?

The Bible consistently demonstrates that those who fear God, live righteously, and place their faith and trust in Him receive promotion. It is a spiritual principle that when people honor God with their lives, they become aligned with God's will and they are favored for promotion. It is not about one's personal achievements or human accolades, but rather their submission and obedience to God.

When Does God Promote?

Based on biblical teachings, God promotes when His timing is right, not our own. God's timing for promotion is perfect and divine, not bound by human standards and expectations. His clock is set by external purposes and not by earthly timelines. Therefore, the Bible notes that the believer must remain patient and persistent in prayer, faith, and good deeds, and in God's appropriate time, the promotion will come.

Where Does Promotion Come From in the Bible?

The Bible demonstrates that promotion comes from God alone. While people, circumstances, or qualifications may seem to be the immediate cause for promotion, the Word asserts that they are simply tools in God's hand. Promotion is treated not as a cause but as an effect of God's favor above earthly favor.

How Should We Handle Promotion According to the Bible?

The Bible advises individuals to handle promotion with humility, acknowledging that it is God's blessing and favor that brought them to higher positions. Believers are encouraged to use any position of authority or influence to serve others and advance God's kingdom on earth. The Bible also advises against using one's position for personal advantage and encourages using such opportunities for the glorification of God, the service of others and the spreading of the gospel message.

Chapter 3
Leadership Role

"And He gave some apostles, and some prophets and some evangelists and some pastors and teachers."
Ephesians 4:11 KJV

In the New Testament letter known as Ephesians, we find a short list of what might be called, "leadership roles" in the church. The word "leadership" does not appear in this passage; neither does the word "roles." What we do read is this:

"So, Christ Himself gave the apostles, the prophets, the evangelists, the pastors and teachers to equip his people for works of service, so that the body of Christ may be built up."
Ephesians 4:11-12

As we read this passage, we wonder about the roles mentioned. What exactly were the apostles, prophets, evangelists, pastors and teachers? What exactly did they do? How is this relevant to the church today?

Commentors, preachers and teachers have proposed various answers to these questions. There have been debates about whether all these roles belong in the church today, or whether apostles and prophets were only for the early church. Many have tried to define the precise function of each role. Some have built elaborate missions and models based on the five-fold ministry of Ephesians 4:11. The main problem with these sincere efforts is that Ephesians 4 gives us so little to go on. This passage does not explain the distinctive work of each role, only what they have in common, namely their sources and their purpose.

We can fashion, however, a rough idea of the roles mentioned in verse 11. Apostles were authorized and sent to preach the gospel and to plant, nurture, and oversee churches. Prophets communicated God's truth to God's people, not only concerning the future (1 Corinthians 14:1-40). The meaning of the word "evangelist" suggests that this role had a responsibility to share the gospel with those who had not received it. Pastors were those who oversaw and cared for God's flock, much like literal shepherds with their sheep. In fact, the Greek word translated here as "pastor" means "shepherd." In the New Testament, it is used in the sense of "pastor" for people, only here, except for passages that speak of Jesus as the shepherd of His flock (John 10:11-16, Hebrews 13:20, 1 Peter 2:25). Finally, teachers instructed God's people in God's truth.

The various roles mentioned in Ephesians 4:11 overlap considerably. Take Paul for example; he was an

Apostle (Ephesians 1:1), yet he also evangelized (1 Cor 1:17), taught (Col. 1:28) and exercised pastoral oversight of his churches (1 Thess. 1:5). Moreover, it is likely that Paul prophesied (1 Cor 13:2, 14:3-6,33). Furthermore, the Greek language used in Ephesians 4:11 suggests a strong connection between the role of pastor and teacher. A literal translation of this verse reads," (Christ gave) the apostles, the prophets, the evangelists, the shepherds and teachers." While the absence of the definite article in front of "teachers" might be stylistic, it seems more likely that Paul regarded the functions of pastor and teacher as inextricably linked. The emphasis in our passage, at any rate, is not on the distinctions between the roles but rather on what they share in common. The are all gifts from Christ to the church.

So, all of the "leadership" roles mentioned in Ephesians 4:11 have a common source, Christ. They also have a common purpose, which appears in verse 12,

"to equip His people for works of service so that the body of Christ may be built up."

Ephesians 4:12

The translation "works of service," strangely obscures the meaning of the original Greek text, which reads literally, "a/the works of ministry." Ministry is not something done only by the apostles, prophets, evangelists, pastors and teachers.

Rather, their job is to equip all of God's people for ministry, and this ministry will build up the body of Christ, that is, the church. However, we understand the different leadership roles of Ephesians 4; what is clear is that they all come from Christ and are given to the church to equip Christ's people for ministry. As we seek to make connections between the leaders in Ephesians 4 and those in the church today, we might say the same things about what matters most. Church leaders are gifts from Christ to the church, and no matter their roles, they all should contribute to the equipping of God's people for the ministry.

Chapter 4

The Apostolic Mantle

"You have made him to have dominion over the works of your hands."

Not every saint who has an anointing to hear the voice of God and speak His purposes is called as a Prophet, however every believer can function under a prophetic anointing, moving in the gifts of the Holy Spirit and operating under the mantle of revelation. In the same manner, not all who lay foundations of reform or do signs and wonders are called to be Apostles but are all called to be apostolically sent into our places of influence with the apostolic anointing to challenge people to change.

The word, "Apostle," in the New Testament means "sent one." The early Apostles changed cities and nations as they were sent by God, with the gospel message and demonstration of power. An apostolic mantle carries an anointing to build the body of Christ upon firm foundations.

Therefore, [a]holy brothers and sisters, who share in the heavenly calling, [thoughtfully and attentively] consider the Apostle and High Priest whom we confessed [as ours when we accepted Him as Savior], namely, [b]Jesus; 2 He

was faithful to Him who appointed Him [Apostle and High Priest], as Moses also was *faithful* in all God's house. ³ Yet Jesus has been considered worthy of much greater glory *and* honor than Moses, just as the builder of a house has more honor than the house. ⁴ For every house is built by someone, but the builder of all things is God. ⁵ Now Moses was faithful in [the administration of] all God's house, [but only] as a *ministering* servant, [his ministry serving] as a testimony of the things which were to be spoken afterward [the revelation to come in Christ]; ⁶ but Christ is faithful as a Son over His [Father's] house. And we are His house if we hold fast our confidence and sense of triumph in our hope [in Christ].

HEBREWS 3:1-6

Those with an apostolic mantle challenged mindsets of the past and speak words of truth — setting the church free to step into their destiny.

⁴² They were continually *and* faithfully devoting themselves to the instruction of the apostles, and to fellowship, to [a]eating meals together and to prayers.

Acts 2:42

And for this matter I was appointed a preacher and an apostle—I am telling the truth, I am not lying [when I say this]—a teacher of the Gentiles in faith and truth.

1 Tim 2:7

They challenge dead religious patterns, destructive mindsets of limitations and oppressive systems that keep God's kingdom from growing. They rise up and build – they impart wisdom and insight into the generations. They are bridge builders between generations, ministries, leaders, businesses, and nations. They connect disjointed parts through relationships, release vision and gather and construct an inheritance for the next generation of people and resources. Apostolic people have an equipping anointing. They fully equip the body of Christ for the work of the ministry. The apostolic anointing desires to see the saints grow from spiritual childhood to maturity.

Evangelists: equip the church to win soul
Teachers: equip the church to make other disciples
Pastors: equip the church to nurture, care and counsel believers
Prophets: equip the church to hear the voice of God and speak for His purposes.
Apostles: Equip the church with wisdom, divine strategies and demonstration of power.

25

An Apostolic mantle has an anointing for leadership — full of wisdom and strategy, a capacity to lay hold of vision and the divine strategies that must be implemented for breakthrough. They have governmental authority and anointing. They are not afraid to step up to the plate and deal with difficult issues that immobilize the church. They carry an ability to face difficult issues with wisdom and are anointed to gather, inspire motivate and mobilize. They know that they can stand in a place of greater authority because they have learned to be under authority. Apostolic people walk in the same governmental authority that the early Apostles did in Acts 16:4.

Apostolic people are reformers. They improve or amend that which is wrong, corrupt or unsatisfactory. Reform means, "the amendment of conduct or belief to change to a better state or form, to cause a person to abandon wrong or evil ways of conduct; to put to end abuses and disorders." Apostolic people are pioneers who are not afraid to challenge the way things have always been done. They think outside the box and hate the spirit of religion; they are trailblazers who are willing to listen to the Lord for new strategies and implement new ideas that will facilitate increase and expansion. They shift the source of history. The Apostolic mantle is a mantle of great grace (Acts 4:33). The church will thrive in times of persecution due in part to God's anointing of great grace that will rest upon His people. This mantle has an anointing to release God's favor into situations to bring freedom and life.

Chapter 5

Lay Hands on No Man Suddenly

22 Do not hurry to lay hands on anyone [ordaining and approving someone for ministry or an office in the church, or in reinstating expelled offenders], and thereby share in the sins of others; keep yourself free from sin.

1 TIM 5:22 AMP

No car manufacturer would release a new model car to the public without first testing the weaknesses and strengths of that automobile. To test the new model, the manufacturer will order it to be driven as fast as possible and will be crashed into a wall and even driven over nails to test for its durability and protection. It will be driven over every conceivable kind of pavement and in all kinds of temperatures. Only after the car passes the final inspection will it be deemed "fit" for public usage. To release a car without this level of testing and examination would be considered irresponsible. If the manufacturer does not test a new model, how can he know whether it will perform well? How can he know whether or not it has fatal mistakes in its structure? How can he know for sure that it will not kill someone? The manufacturer is well aware that if they release the car to the public and it falls apart or kills someone, they will be held responsible for that failure. New automobiles are tested to protect people from being physically hurt in automobile accidents. But what about testing potential leaders before giving them highly visible places of power and authority in a church, business or organization?

People are precious to God, and they should be precious to us as well. But before we give people great power and authority in a church or an organization, they first need to be tested and proven. It is essential that those of us who are in leadership positions know who these individuals really are and how they will perform in various situations.

The Apostle Paul referred to this testing process when he wrote, "Lay hands suddenly on no man neither be a partaker of other men's sins, keep thyself pure." (1 Tim 5:22) The word "suddenly" is the Greek word "tachus", and in this verse it carries the idea of doing something quickly and hastily. The word "lay hands" are from the Greek work "epitithimi" which means "to place hands upon us." In both the Old Testament and the New Testament times, a "laying on of hands" ceremony was the equivalent of stamping that individual with one's personal seal of approval. When those in leadership positions lay hands on a person, they were signifying that they believed in him, supported him, and desired to empower him to perform some tasks of duty. Hence, the laying on of hands was an act that was carried out very cautiously, since it gave the recipient such a high status in the eyes of the beholder.

A better translation would be "don't give your seal of approval to people to hastily." You see, it is very possible to lay hands on people too quickly or to give them the seal of our approval before we really know them and to impart authority to them before they are ready. This is a foolish mistake that produces painful consequences. If you feel that God has chosen you, do not get frustrated if you are held back for a while from those who are in authority over you. It is wise and right for them to know you, test you, and be sure that you are the right candidate for the job. If God has really chosen you, it will not hurt you or the call He has placed on your life to wait just a little bit longer. If anything, your divine call will be confirmed and reconfirmed again and again as you patiently wait for God's timing to be manifested.

When I was a young man, I had desire, ambition and the necessary "get up and go" to do what God had placed on my heart. But there were characteristics in me that needed to be corrected before God could use me. If I had gotten started before God uprooted those undesirable traits they would have later overgrown my ministry and destroyed any fruitfulness God wanted to produce through me. This is why it is an aspect of immaturity to want to do everything right now. If you are the one who chooses the leadership for your church, ministry or organization, do not move hastily! Nothing is more

31

important in your organization than the people you choose for its leadership. If you choose people who share your heart and are submitted to you and your vision, they will be a blessing. But if you choose people who have a different vision and are not in agreement with what God has put in your heart, you have invited a spiritual hurricane into your midst that has the power to destroy everything you have built. A note for you - take time to be sure that you are making the right decision.

We all have glitches and flaws in our character, not one of us is perfect. Fortunately, small flaws are correctable as long as we have receptive and teachable hearts. But if a person refuses to see his need for change and is closed-hearted to suggestions made by those who love him — this is evidence of the most serious character flaw. From the outside, this person may look like "he is just the one we are looking for," but we must not forget to consider the deeper issues of the heart.

Pastors and leaders of ministries and organizations can attest to the dreadful mistake of "laying hands on people" before they were ready. Most leaders could tell you about people they promoted into leadership too quickly before they really knew them. These are the people who often betrayed their leaders, split their churches, divided their organizations and wounded those leader's spirits so deeply that it took a long time for them to recuperate and return to a state of normalcy again in their lives and ministries. Often the hurt a person causes in such a case is unintentional. He or she was simply not ready for that much power and authority, and to think that the whole mess could have been avoided if more time had been taken before the person was elevated to a leadership position! Many dreadful mistakes have been made though two thousand years of church history simply because people were placed into leadership positions too quickly. Had time been taken and had those people really been tested, it would have been clear that they were not spiritually prepared to lead. But as a result of hasty decisions and quick actions, multitudes of people have been mishandled and hurt by immature leadership.

Don't make the same mistake! Before someone is invited to be a permanent part of any leadership team, it is right to make sure that there is nothing in his character, attitude or actions that could spiritually hurt others or the organization along the way. Remember, you are putting this potential leader over people and nothing in the world is more valuable or precious than the people of God. You don't want to make a hasty decision that reaps terrible consequences for your church, ministry or organization.

Paul told Timothy that by not laying hands on people too quickly, he could avoid being a "partaker of other men's sins." The word "partaker" is the Greek word "Koinonia" which conveys the ideas of fellowship, interaction or mutual participation. If you are in a leadership position, take time to know someone before you give that person new power and authority. If you are wanting to be chosen for a higher position yourself, be patient with those who are waiting and watching you. They have a God-given responsibility to know you and feel confident about you before they lay hands on you!

Finally, pray for your pastor or employer to make right decisions about people they promote into leadership positions in their church, business, or organization. They need your prayers of support, so get behind them with your prayers today!

My Prayer for Today

Lord, you know me better than anyone in the world. I trust you to know exactly when I am ready for the next big promotion that you have designed for my life. Help me to quit being frustrated with my superiors for not promoting me more quickly and help me instead to take a look at the deeper issues of my life that hold me back from being elevated. Holy Spirit, help me use this time in my life to clean up my act and get my heart ready for the next upward step that Jesus has waiting for me! I pray this in Jesus' name, AMEN!

My Confession for Today

I confess that my character, attitude and actions are being refined by the fire of God in my life. The Holy Spirit is helping me to discover any serious character flaws that would negatively affect my future. God is changing me, teaching me and preparing me for greater responsibility. I am serious about my walk with God and about being greatly used by Him in this life. Therefore, I want Him to identify every part of my life that is out of order and needs to be fixed. Today I yield to the Holy Spirit so He can delve deep into my soul and extract those traits that would keep me from the blessings and positions God would love to give me.

I declare this by faith, in Jesus' name!

Chapter 6

Unprocessed Ministers

"For he is the minister of God to thee for good. But, if thou do that which is evil, be afraid, for he beareth not the sword in vain."

Romans 13:4

Are you unprocessed? Just in a hurry to become a minister in the gospel of Jesus Christ? You feel you're called but deep down inside you're not ready but instead take the approach and say these famous words, "I'll fake it until I make it"? Here's the harsh truth about ministry. For starters for someone who is called to ministry, working another job will be miserable. For someone not called to ministry, working in ministry, will be equally miserable.

How do you know that you have been called to ministry? Charles Spurgeon said that the sign of God's call to ministry was an,

"intense, all absorbing desire for the work."

You can probably track down even more people who think this way. The call to full time Christian ministry has always been described as a mystical call from God that cannot be explained. Someone who is called to the ministry senses that God wishes for him or her to devote their life to serving in the local church or abroad.

How does God call us to serve?

What should you do when God calls you to ministry?

Here are a few practical suggestions.

1. Be honest about your desires. (Psalm 37:4). God will give you the desires of your heart. It is not humble to be silent about the dreams God has placed in your heart.
2. Interpret your desires as a mandate to prepare and not a license to launch.
3. Make sure you have a place where your burden can be evaluated.
4. Remember that calling is revealed in service.

What should you do if you feel you are called to ministry?

Remember first and foremost, it is not humble to be silent about the dreams that God has placed in your heart. If you are going to go forth in ministry whether it is at your local church, hospital or even prison ministry, you need to let others know about the desires stirring in your heart. If you sense the call to ministry, humbly share your thoughts and dreams with your pastor.

> "Interpret your desires as a mandate to prepare and not a license to launch."

In this book I have described and will continue to describe many development phases that leaders go through. In the first three phases, God is working primarily in the leader, not through the leader. God is so passionate about His people that He will take the necessary time to forge the character of a man before putting that man in a position of leadership. Do not be preoccupied with your age. Time is not passing you by - if God wants you to be in ministry nothing including the passing of time can stop Him. Remember this,

"the greatest and hardest preparation is within."

Make sure you have a place where your burden can be elevated.

We tend to assign a unique authority to our subjective impressions about our calling, as if our sense of calling is divinely inspired and untouchable. This should not be the case.

Rather a sense of call to ministry must be evaluated through God's Word and wise counsel. It is important to understand the nature of burdens. A burden for ministry is an invitation before it is an engine.

1. **A burden is a mandate to pray before it is a mandate to go.**
2. **A burden is a mandate to pursue council before it is a mandate to go.**
3. **A burden is a mandate to pursue evaluation before it is a mandate to go.**
4. **A burden is a mandate to apply before it is a mandate to go.**

So many ministers intend on doing something, but forget that God's main work is to make something of them!

Remember that calling is revealed in service.

The most important thing is not to discover your role, but instead, in God's eyes, to serve. In Mark 10:42, Jesus said,

"you know that those who are considered rulers of the gentiles lord it over them, and their great ones exercise authority over them, but not so with you.

Whoever would be great must first become a servant."

If you sense a call to ministry, invite others into your life, allow your call to be evaluated, and dive into serving at your local church.

Misdiagnosed 101

Most of you reading this book will assume, "if I am called to the ministry, then I must be reminded of this one simple thing - Isaiah was called to be a prophet to Judah, Jonah was called to prophecy to Nineveh, Peter was called to preach to the Gentiles." Most will involuntarily nod in agreement. I myself had nodded in agreement until I realized that, "Paul was not called to the Gentiles, Jonah was not called to go to Nineveh, Peter was not called to preach to the Gentiles." While each of the statements may challenge your thoughts and understanding, the truth is that each of them are true nonetheless. The truth is that throughout the entire Bible, people are called to one and only one thing, or relationship with God. Look it up for yourself, here are just a few."

"I press on toward the goal for the reward of the upward calling of God in Christ Jesus."

Philippians 3:14

"He has saved us and called us with a holy calling, not because of our deeds but because of his own purpose and grace."

2 Timothy 1:9

"Therefore brothers and sisters, make all the more effort to make your calling and election sure."

2 Peter 1:10

"God is faithful, through whom you were called into the fellowship of his son, Jesus our Lord."

1 Corinthians 1:9

When someone is called, it causes them to draw nearer to the collar. When someone is sent, it causes them to go away from the one sending them. When we focus too much on what we are sent to do, we can quickly get so busy doing that, and therefore, fail to remember our calling. Our purpose and goal become our ministry rather than the call. Because we are constantly told that our calling is our ministry, we begin to draw near to our ministry instead of drawing near to our God. We see what happens to those who forget that their ministry is not their calling every time we see someone in ministry fall because of pride and arrogance. When we falsely believe that our calling is our ministry, then our ministry becomes about us. When we remember that our only calling is to draw near to God, then we will always remember that even while we are doing what He sent us to do, everything we are doing while we are sent has to be focused and purposed to help us draw nearer to Him.

It is only when we fully embrace Our Calling to draw near to God, that we can be eligible to respond to the words,

"whom should I send, and who will go for us?", with these words, "Hineni. Send me." (Here I am, send me.)

When we understand what our calling is, then we can fulfill the Great Commission by going into all the world preaching the good news as we read in Matthew 11:28.

Chapter 7
Rebellious Elders

"Is there any sick among you? Let him call for the elders of the church, and let them pray over him, anointing him with oil in the name of the Lord."

James 5:14-16

I can relate to this title and anointing of that of an Elder. I never will forget the years I spent as an Elder under Bishop Clyde Sellers of Faith Worship Believers Church. It was a humbling experience. One thing I can remember in my vocation of eldership is that of hospitality ministry.

I remember the many times that my Bishop at the time would show me the in's and out's of hospital ministry. This area of service allowed me to focus on prayer and the power of God and on how He will heal the sick and the shut in. Even today as a Bishop myself, I will never forget the times and experiences I had as I walked as an Elder in the Lord's church. Even until this day, many of the old members I once shared fellowship with under Bishop Sellers still refer to me as and call me Elder.

"Despise not small beginnings."

Zechariah 4:10

I will never forget my walk as Elder Adkins some ten to twelve years ago. It is my prayer today that whoever is seeking eldership, I ask that you embrace it even the more.

"Is anyone among you sick? Then he must call for the elders of the church and they are to pray over him, anointing him with oil in the name of the Lord."

James 5:14 (NASB)

Praying in Faith

Prayer is a great privilege for the Christian, for it affords us with an audience at the throne of grace, for mercy to find help in time of need. The book of James both begins and ends with the prayer of faith. At the beginning, we are warned against being a double minded Christian, where we pray with doubt in our hearts and right at the end of his letter, we discover the effective, fervent prayer of the righteous man, has its roots and trust in God and believing His word.

The final section of the epistle to James encourages prayer in times of suffering, and times of rejoicing, and also in times of sickness. No matter what we are facing, we are not only encouraged to pray for ourselves and others, but also instructed to ask for prayer, when we ourselves are in need. In this verse James asks and then answers his own question.

"Is anyone among you sick? Then he must call for the elders of the church and they are to pray for him, anointing him with oil in the name of the Lord."

Allow a brief teaching moment. What is James describing here? Ready? The anointing of a sick body was indeed a medical practice during the times of Christ, and God often combines natural medication with supernatural healing, but James clearly is identifying illness, an anointing oil in verse 14 with an illness and the prayer of faith in verse 15. James' instruction to both the sick person and the church elders is simply an outward demonstration of an inward call. This passage is notoriously enigmatic, and I certainly do not have the final word on it. But since it seems to answer the question proposed, it is worth considering how this text should shape ministry to the sick in our congregations. I have no intention of untying every exegetical knot (there are many). Instead, I hope we can get a general idea of what James is commending by simply asking questions of the text and following the basic hermeneutical principle that we should always let clearer parts of the scripture guide and constrain our interpretations of more difficult passages like this one.

With that throat clearing out of the way, let's consider four questions that help us understand what Jesus is commending.

1. Should we apply this passage to every sickness?

James is not suggesting that you get on the phone with your elders and ask them to break out the oil every time your seasonal allergies act up or you get the sniffles. The fact that the sick person in this text has to "call for" the elders to visit him, suggest that the person is significantly ill and unable to attend corporate gatherings or other functions where they might encounter the elders. Further, the description of healing suggests that the illness is severe.

2. Why should the sick call on the elders?

Pragmatically, calling your elders to pray for you in time of sickness puts your needs not only before them, but likely before the whole congregation. As the shepherds of your church, the elders are best suited to know how to care for you, how to express your needs to the church, and how to minister the hope of the gospel.

> **Faith theology isn't an enterprise on following feelings or intuition. It is a matter of submitting to scripture wherever it leads.**

The end of verse 16 may provide another clue as to why the six should call on their elders to pray for them. In that verse, James teaches that "the prayer of the righteous person has great power as it is working." Given the qualifications for elders (1 Timothy 3:1-7), and their responsibility to model godliness for the congregation (1 Peter 5:3), the elders in your church should be above reproach and you should invite their intercession. Notably, James indicates that the sick man initiates contact with the elders and asks for prayer and anointing. These are acts of faith and humility on his part, expressions of humble reliance on the God who holds the power of life and death in His hands.

3. What's the deal with the oil?

James' mention of oil is certainly one of the most enigmatic parts of the passage. Let's rule out what anointing oil doesn't mean.

First, James is not teaching the Roman Catholic doctrine of extreme unction. He nowhere indicates that we should see anointing the sick with oil as "sacrament." Furthermore, the use of oil in this passage is not to prepare the sick for death but is appended to the prayers that look for healing and restoration. Second, James is not suggesting that the oil bears any mystical, magical, or supernatural quality. The healing results from the elders praying, "in the name of the Lord." The oil is secondary in this passage, adorning the central act of prayer. Finally, the oil in this passage is not medicinal, as some may suggest. While an intriguing proposal, there is no evidence in this test that "oil" should be read as a stand in for medicine. In fact, in Mark 6:13, the only other time we find oil and healing connected in the New Testament, oil is clearly not medicinal, since the healings described in that passage are supernatural.

So, what's the point of anointing with oil? Likely, anointing with oil simply symbolizes consecration to God, as often does elsewhere in scripture. (Numbers 3:3, 1 Samuel 10:1, Psalm 89:20). Anointing with oil is a physical way of expressing a spiritual truth.

4. Does this passage promise those anointed will be healed without exception as long as they have enough faith?

The beginning of verse 15 seems to suggest that "prayers of faith" inevitably result in physical healing. Certainly, such an interpretation does not accord with reality. Godliness is not a guarantee of physical health, nor can it perpetually deter death (Hebrews 9:27.) Furthermore, Paul himself, perhaps the most faithful Christian ever, had to leave Trophimus sick in Miletus. (2 Timothy 4:20.) Remember, praying and faith is not a magical formula that twists God's arm to do what we want. Rather, praying in faith both boldly asks God to heal a sick brother or sister and humbly trust God's perfect plan.

Humble reliance on God's mercy

Should we anoint the sick with oil? It depends on the situation. On the other hand, God does not command Christians to seek out every sick brother or sister and anoint them. But if someone seriously ill desires healing, then yes one way they can express their wholehearted reliance and submission to God is by asking righteous men to intercede for them and symbolize their commitment to the Lord by being anointed with oil.

Chapter 8

Fruitless Pastors

"God gives Pastors after His own heart."

Jeremiah 3:15

> **Pastor: "a minister in charge of a Christian church or congregation."**

A pastor is the leader of a Christian congregation who also gives advice and counsel to people from the community or congregation. Pastors are always ordained. Pastors may either be licensed or ordained.

Most people who have a good word for their people, who may be able to preach good tidings, does not necessarily mean that they have been called to pastor. Preaching is proclaiming Jesus, therefore, we must not confuse pastoring with preaching. Anyone can preach but not everyone can or should pastor (Ephesians 4:11), as God gave "some."

Some means "not all"! That is why today in many churches and in many denominations, we have fruitless pastors - those with no fruit, no substance, only a good word.

What is the meaning of a Pastor?

Pastors lead church services and help others worship. "Pastor" is a religious title used mostly in Christian churches. They are leaders within a church who have been ordained and therefore given the authority to conduct religious services. A Pastor is a Christian who walks with God in their personal life. They feel that they are called to serve others in their spiritual and physical needs as ministers. This inner calling speaks to their soul. They believe it is God calling them to service.

What is a pastor according to the Bible?

A pastor is a leader. His or her function is to lead the church. Paul told Timothy that a Pastor must be able to "manage" the church (1 Timothy 3:5). Paul uses an interesting term for "manage." The term that Paul uses speaks of a house manager.

What is a Pastor versus a preacher?

We refer to a person who delivers a Sunday message as a preacher. We call the person that is chosen to lead the church, the pastor. We typically regard a missionary as someone who leaves the comfort of home and travels abroad to bring the gospel to those of another culture; therefore, we use these words as titles.

What do Pastors actually do?

A Pastor is also called a minister or a vicar, who tends to the spiritual warfare of a Christian congregation or church. This often includes preaching and teaching from the bible and providing counsel primarily to those within the congregation. A Pastor may be a part of a ministerial team or a may have a senior leadership role.

How does God call a pastor?

First and foremost, one must understand and know how to identify the voice of God.

"And the child Samuel ministered unto the Lord before Eli. And the word of the Lord was precious in those days, there was no open vision. And it came to pass at that time when Eli was laid down in his place, and his eyes began to wax dim, that he could not see. And ere The lamp of God went out in the temple of the Lord, where the ark of God was, and Samuel laid down to sleep. That the Lord called Samuel, and he answered," here am I."

1 Samuel 3:1-4

One must know and recognize the voice of God in order to hearken to His directions and instructions. Remember it was Noah in Genesis chapter 6 that heard God to build an ark (the specifics were to build an ark out of Gopher wood).

It was Abraham who heard God for his blessings in Genesis 12 to move from where he was and to go to a land which God would show him in order to bless him. We must hear God so that we can move forward into what He has ordained for our lives. We can hear God differently than the norm; we hear Him through spirit. God speaks to those persons He has called to serve as Pastors and ministers of His church. The great reformer Martin Luther described this inward call as, "God's voice heard by faith." Those whom God has called know this call by a sense of leading purpose and growing commitment.

Understanding the call to Pastoral ministry

Pastors are church leaders, and their responsibilities include providing spiritual guidance and counseling for congregation.

Who qualifies as a pastor?

Most Christian denominations require a pastor to have an education in theology and biblical studies.

How to be a pastor:
Qualifications and steps to become a pastor

Do you feel the call to ministry? Becoming a pastor is a noble and fulfilling call that requires a deep understanding of the scriptures, as well as the skills and attitude to guide and care for our congregation. While the path to becoming a pastor may vary, there are certain qualifications and steps one can take to prepare for a career in ministry. In this chapter we will explore the steps you can take to become a Pastor and discuss the importance of acquiring pastoral skills to serve both the congregation and the community effectively.

Qualifications and skills needed to become a pastor

1. Tending to the congregation.

A pastor should have a sense of responsibility for the well-being of their congregation. They should develop both spiritual and physical well-being of their flock, understanding their challenges and offering support.

2. Instruction and guidance

Pastors must have the theological knowledge and training to guide their congregation according to the doctrine of the church. They are responsible for delivering relevant and accurate sermons, setting the curriculum for Bible studies and Sunday school, and providing guidance in the matter of faith.

3. Care and compassion

Showing understanding, compassion, and providing care to those in need is a crucial aspect of pastoral work. Pastors should offer support to individuals experiencing pain, provide counseling and times of need, and be a source of comfort and guidance during challenging life circumstances.

4. Leadership

Pastors are leaders in both administrative and moral aspects. They make decisions for their church, manage day-to-day tasks, and oversee the overall function of the organization. Additionally, pastors must demonstrate moral leadership by upholding the teachings of the scriptures and leading by example.

A step-by-step breakdown on becoming a pastor

Becoming a pastor is a unique and spiritual journey that involves both personal growth and acquiring knowledge. Here's a breakdown of the journey to becoming a pastor.

1. Volunteer for servicing your church.

Start by getting involved in your own church community. Volunteer for various roles such as late preacher, Sunday school teacher, or Bible study leader. This will allow you to test your abilities, gain experience, and receive feedback from others. Engage in mentorship and seek guidance through prayer as you serve your community.

2. Get a complete education and religion and pastoral studies.

Most Christian denominations require pastors to have an education in theology and biblical studies. Pursue a theology degree, Christian studies, or Divinity at a college or university. Bachelor's degree in religious studies or theology often include courses in literature, art, mathematics, social studies, history and languages. Additionally, you will study subjects like biblical studies, theology, comparative religion, Christian history, and philosophy. Consider specializing in a specific area of pastoral studies through concentrations such as biblical studies, philosophy, youth ministry, pastoral studies, or Christian education.

3. Seek ordination and begin ministry.

Once you have fulfilled the requirements of your denomination, including completing your education, you can seek ordination as a Pastor. Ordination represents the official recognition of your call to ministry and the authorization to act as a minister of your faith. With your ordination you can begin your ministry and serve as a Pastor in a church or other religious organization. Remember that the specific process may vary depending on the denomination and individual circumstances it is essential to consult with your church and denomination for detailed guidance on your specific path to becoming a pastor.

What are three words to describe a pastor?

We are not only talking about those who serve as the Pastor of the local churches but all of those who serve as spiritual leaders of groups of believers. In Acts 20 and 1 Peter 5, we see the three terms of shepherd, elder and overseer use interchangeably to describe the way in which these spiritual leaders lead.

Is being a pastor a gift?

Among those gifts, Ephesians 4:11 states that the Holy Spirit gives some of the members of the body of Christ the grace, power and authority to serve as pastors. As such, service as a pastor is first and foremost a spiritual gift rather than a mere profession or office.

What is the job of a pastor according to the Bible?

He or she is a steward and a manager of God's resources and Jesus' flock. He takes responsibility, but not ownership. A pastor must be humble, and not arrogant (Titus 1:7). A pastor must constantly demonstrate the gospel by admitting when he is wrong and assuming responsibility and restoring relationships. A pastor must aim at four primary responsibilities in the pastoral work:

1. Preaching and teaching the word.

2. Shepherding or caring for God's people.

3. Stewardship of the resources of the church.

4. Being an example to the flock.

Understand this - a pastor must proclaim the Word as well as explain the word in teaching. Paul tells Titus, "proclaim the word with all authority and let no one circumvent that." We have one primary task and that is to take the word of God and disseminate it to the people of God and then to the world. We are above all things, preachers.

Being a pastor comes with ups and downs. I guess that is why the Apostle Paul says to be constant in and out of season (2 Timothy 4:2). We are to reprove, rebuke and exhort, with all suffering and doctrine. As pastors we should know that we are accountable to the almighty God for how we teach and lead the church which suggests that we as spiritual leaders must and will give an account for the souls of the people we lead.

What is the main purpose of a Pastor?

First, to help the church members discover their spiritual gifts. These gifts can be defined as a "special ability given by God's grace to enhance the work of God's Kingdom." Second, to start needed ministries within the church and community. Lastly the role of a Pastor is to recruit the appropriate gifts to the appropriate ministry. Remember when it comes to being a pastor, the Apostle Paul reminds us in Ephesians 4:11 that "He gave some." Remember, everyone is not a pastor.

Chapter 9

The Evangelist

"But you, keep your head in all situations, endure hardship, do the work of an evangelist, discharge all the duties of your ministry."

2 Timothy 4:5

Evangelist: "a person who seeks to convert others to the Christian faith, especially by public preaching."

What is the real meaning of an Evangelist? An Evangelist is a person who travels from place to place in an effort to convert people to Christianity.

What is the job of an evangelist?

Evangelists are often known for their powerful preaching and public speaking abilities. They may preach in a variety of settings, such as churches, outdoor events, or revival meetings. Evangelists share the gospel. The primary role of an Evangelist is to share the gospel of Jesus Christ according to Titus 2:11. There are four essential doctrines and to be saved a person must have a "born again conversion" experience, hence evangelicals are also known as born again Christians.

Who qualifies to be an evangelist?

The minimum qualification to become an evangelist is being a licensed or ordained minister of the Christian faith.

What is the difference between an evangelist and a preacher?

Preaching is the act or practice of delivering public discourses or addresses on moral and religious subjects, and the delivery of sermons. Evangelism is the telling of the "good news", or the promulgation of the gospel.

What is the role of an evangelist?

The role of an evangelist is to spread the Christian gospel and message of salvation to others, often with the goal of leading them to a personal relationship with Jesus Christ. Evangelists are typically associated with the Protestant tradition of Christianity and are considered to have a gift or calling for evangelism.

Some specific roles and responsibilities of an evangelist may include:

1. **Preaching:** Evangelists are often known for their powerful preaching and public speaking abilities.

They may preach in a variety of settings, such as churches, outdoor events, or revival meetings.

2. **Sharing the Gospel:** the primary role of an Evangelist is to share the good news of Jesus Christ with others. This may involve one-on-one conversations or conversions, small group discussions, or large-scale events.

3. **Discipleship:** Evangelists may also play a role in discipling new believers, helping them grow in their faith and develop a deeper understanding of the Bible and Christian principles.

4. **Outreach and Missions:** Many Evangelists are involved in outreach and mission work, both locally and globally. This may involve supporting missionaries, providing aid and assistance to those in need, or spreading the gospel in areas where it is not widely known or accepted.

Overall, the role of an evangelist is to share the gospel message of salvation and invite others into a personal relationship with Jesus Christ. They may do this through preaching, teaching, mentoring, and outreach activities, working to bring others closer to God and share God's word.

The Evangelist

The Apostle Paul told his son in ministry "do the work of an evangelist", but exactly what is an evangelist?

The word "euaggelistori" means "one who proclaims the glad tidings."

In that sense, anyone who brings good news to another is an Evangelist. The concept that one who is called into itinerant evangelism cannot also possess the heart of a Pastor or the mind of a scholar is unbiblical. The Evangelist is to be a bearer of the glad tidings of Jesus Christ whether he serves an itinerant evangelism, the pastorate, the classroom or some other God called vocation. Every born-again child of God is an evangelist if we take the Great Commission seriously.

The Apostle Paul charged Timothy to "preach the word!" Be ready in season and out of season, convince, rebuke, exhort, with all long-suffering and teaching." This is the work of the evangelist. He or she is to faithfully proclaim the unsearchable riches of Christ, to make the center aware of his sins, to correct with compassion, to encourage with hope and to never lose hope in or belief that man is beyond redemption. This can only be done and accomplished when one is willing to fulfill his ministry. Keep in mind, Paul challenges young Timothy to be faithful in four basic areas in fulfilling his work as an evangelist - hold sound doctrine, teach sound doctrine, continue in sound doctrine, and preach sound doctrine.

Those words of spirit anointed counsel ring as true today as when Paul first pinned them from his prison headquarters in Rome. As ambassadors of the great doctrines, it is also our responsibility, whether in the role of Evangelist or Pastor, to be aware of the signs of the time. Paul told young Timothy, "know this, that in the last days perilous times will come." It seems that the history of the church has gone from unity to division where being in one accord was the staple characteristic in the early church and has now become non-existent. It now appears that discord is often associated with trying to fulfill our ministry. Not only are mainline denominations splitting up over doctrinal issues, but many individual churches seem to be adrift in a sea of uncertainty and conflict.

Our work as Evangelists and Pastors are to have a single mindedness like the saints who preceded us. Paul instructed Timothy to "do what I told you to do."
Remember, we are not the chef, we are the waiters. Just get the word out of the kitchen and serve it while it is still hot. Single mindedness means to stick to the basics. As preachers of the unsearchable riches, we are not called to be inventors or even innovators. We are called to be proclaimers of what has already been written. It is the working of the basics which will fulfill our ministry and further the Kingdom.

Our work also calls us to preach without apology the salvation of the scriptures. Paul reminded Timothy, "the holy scriptures which are able to be make you wise for salvation." The power of the spoken scriptures is enough to bring down strongholds. It saves to the utmost. It sacrifices. It is all sufficient. It sets men free. Our sermons must be sharpened. An Evangelist or a Pastor who does not like to preach should never draw his sword. Doing the work of Evangelist or Pastor, means we must preach sin as damning and the cross as necessary, the blood is cleansing, the resurrection is fact, and the second coming as expected. It means we must preach the doctrines of the scriptures from, "in the beginning," to "surely, I come quickly." Forget those with itching ears and preach to those with itching hearts. It is not the teaching of fables that will turn the world to Christ. It is however the preaching of the Word by those who are willing to do the work of an Evangelist that will turn many to righteousness.

Remember proverbs 11:30,

"he who wins souls are wise."

Last but not least, evangelist announced good news. The twin words, "euaggelion" meaning "gospel and "euaggelistes" meaning "evangelist," came into biblical use with the advent of Jesus. "Good news" merited "a messenger of good news." The word "evangelist" appears three times in the New Testament, with reference to the person the work and the calling.

Chapter 10
He Gave Some Teachers

"And he gave some apostles, and some prophets, and some evangelists, and some pastors, and some teachers, for the edifying of the body of Christ; till we all come into the unity of the faith and of the knowledge of the son of God, unto a perfect man."

Ephesians 4:1-16

What is a teacher biblically?

A teacher is one who is able to impart truth and wisdom for life. Teaching can take place in different ways but at the end of the day a teacher is one from whom you learn. A teacher from God is one who has divine authority and must be obeyed.

Does God call people to be teachers?

To be called to the teacher is to be chosen by God to serve as a greater purpose serving many people and influencing their development and abilities to positively contribute to their communities.

A teacher from God

"Rabbi, we know you are a teacher who has come from God. For no one could perform the miraculous signs you are doing if God were not with him."

John 3:1-2 (NIV)

Nicodemus recognizes Jesus as a teacher from God. A teacher is one who is able to impart truth and wisdom for life. Teaching can take place in different ways but at the end of the day a teacher is one from whom you learn. A teacher from God is one who has divine authority and must be obeyed. Many churches teach when Nicodemus grasped.

"Jesus is a teacher from God. He has come to show us how to live. We are to walk in the way of Jesus."

Nicodemus grasped all of that. We know that you are our teacher from God we know that you have come to show us how to live God's way, but telling us how to live is something that God had already done. God's people already have the ten commandments, written by the finger of God 1,500 years earlier when Jesus said, "Love God with all your heart and love your neighbor as yourself". He was only repeating what had already been revealed in the Old Testament. To Nicodemus, Jesus is just another teacher like

Moses and the prophets who came from God to tell us what to do. Notice when Nicodemus describes him as a teacher, Jesus does not say, "Nicodemus, you've got it wrong there." He adds to what Nicodemus says but does not take away. No one can claim Christ as Savior who is not ready to submit to Him as Teacher. Christ is never less than a Teacher to His people. He is not less than the law but thank God He is much more.

What is the spiritual gift of teaching?

Teachers usually have the spiritual gifts of prophecy, exhortation, wisdom, knowledge, and discernment. These gifts help them to expand on the scripture and in turn help the church to grow.

"Be diligent to present yourselves approved to God, a worker who does not need to be ashamed, rightly dividing the word of truth."

2 Timothy 2:15

What does Jesus say about teaching?

As the resurrected Lord, Jesus calls upon His followers to make disciples of all people through the preaching of the gospel of the Kingdom. Teaching is a means by which disciples of Jesus are continually transformed in order to become more like Christ. In Matthew 28:16-20, Jesus conveys the Great Commission to his disciples. He says that they have been given authority to disciple others in the name of Christ, and that He expects them to go out and do so.

How to tell if you have the gift of teaching

How can you tell if you have the gift of teaching? First and foremost, one must establish that the teacher is not only a gift but a combination of several gifts; one is the ability to teach from scripture. However, to keep things simple, I will refer to teaching as a "gift". Because it is a blessing, a gift from God, it has been given to certain people to edify the church.

What is the gift of teaching?

The word "dividing" in the Greek is "orthotomeo". Orthos means "straight, right, or proper," and "temno" means, "to cut," the scriptures properly. In other words, those with the gift of teaching will stay straight and true to God's Word. They will not veer from the truth to appease those around them with differing opinions. They will stay focused on context. They will not take one verse and try to make it mean something else. Teachers will not base their Bible studies on revelations, visions, "words of knowledge", or dreams from God, especially if those revelations, visions, etc., cannot be backed up with scripture. Unfortunately, this is a big problem with many celebrity preachers today. Particularly in the Word of Faith Movement and the New Apostolic Reformation

Movement. Both of these groups rely heavily on their "revelations" from God over what the Bible says. A good teacher will keep the Word of God in context. They will consider the whole Word of God and counsel when it's bounding on a particular subject. They do this because scripture does not contradict scripture.

Characteristics of a Teacher

Those who teach will often find themselves digging deeper into scripture and will not be satisfied with meditating only on daily devotions. They want "meat", and will do everything in their power to find those moments in the day when they can spend time in the Word of God. They will often spend hours and sometimes days, preparing lessons because they are cautious with what they teach and how they teach it. Teachers come alive when they can share God is showing them.

Regarding schoolteachers versus Bible teachers, the gift of teaching is not related to the gift schoolteachers have. Many talented schoolteachers have a knack for getting their message across to students. However, you may find those same teachers often flounder when put in position of teaching the Bible. School teachers cannot accurately interpret the scriptures unless they have been given the spiritual gifts of exhortation, discernment, wisdom, knowledge, and prophecy. If you are a schoolteacher and do not feel comfortable teaching Sunday school or Bible study it is likely because God has not called you to lead in that way. Do not let those who think they know best try to convince you otherwise. However, if you are a school teacher who has been given the "gifts of teaching," you, in my humble opinion have been doubly blessed. What a rare treat it would be to have you as a teacher!

Chapter 11
The Prophet

"Houses, cars, money on the way...."

"Surely the Lord will do nothing, but he revealed his secret unto his servants the prophets."

Amos 3:7

One of the most misdiagnosed titles in the church today is that of the Prophet. Everyone swears they are a Prophet. Just because you may have a word of knowledge from time to time does not mean that you are a one. Prophets do not have to play the guessing game; they know for sure because God reveals His secrets to His Prophets. I have come across a lot of them in my life and I can honestly say that the authentic ones I have come across were few and none.

I will say, though, that Prophet Todd Hall is a true Prophet with an amazing gift. Not only can he prophesy like no one's business, but the man can preach, too. I am so glad to have fellowshipped with him on many occasions. During the mini conversations that I was privy to have with him, I was able to glean from his experience and the do's and don'ts of ministry. I have witnessed Prophet Todd Hall on many occasions prophecy and he was right on point! Another Prophet I can say honestly that this happens with is my wife,

Apostle Shaun Adkins. Being married to her for now over ten years, I am privileged to see the prophet in her on a daily basis. She does not miss! If she prophesied to someone and said, "When you get home there will be a 75-inch TV in your backyard," I would tell them to believe every word! When they got home if there is no TV, I would further suggest that they call the police because that meant that they had just been robbed! But on a serious note, not everyone is a Prophet; it is only a gift that was privileged to some and not to all.

We must make our election sure as it states in 2 Peter 1:10-11.

"Wherefore the rather, brethren, give diligence to make your calling and election sure: for if ye do these things, ye shall never fall, for so an entrance shall be ministered unto you abundantly into the everlasting Kingdom of our Lord and savior Jesus Christ."

Who would want to be a Prophet?

By definition, the Prophet has to be on the edge of the inside of institutional religion. It is a hard position to hold, and it must be held both structurally and personally, with wisdom and grace. There are many times it would be easier to leave the system or to play the company man, woman and just go along with the game - Jesus understands this. He loved and respected His Jewish religion, yet He pushed the envelope wide open. He often healed people on the Sabbath which was a deliberate statement against making a practice into a dogma that was higher than human need (Matthew 12:1-8). Yet He honored the same Jewish establishment by telling some He had healed to "go show yourselves to the priests," as stated in Luke 17:14. Jesus walked the thin line of a true Prophet.

Being a Prophet demands two seemingly opposites - radical traditionalism and shocking iconoclasm at the same time. If people could only pick one or the other, they will presume something like this:

"Ohh, he's just a pious little Christian boy," or "she's an angry woman."

They cannot imagine that those two can really coexist, tame, and educate one another. Holding the tension of opposites is the necessary education of the Prophet and the church has given little energy to it. Frankly, it takes nondual thinking to pull this off and we have pretty much trained people in the simplistic choosing of one idealized alternative while disintegrating the other.

To put these two immense opposites demands a great deal of human maturity, the mental realization of being grounded, spiritual intelligence, and readiness to not be liked, even by good people whom you really respect. You must be willing to believe that God is calling you to do this, that God is using you, and that you are an instrument. But please don't believe anyone who is wearing the loud badge of a Prophet; it is never anything anyone should or would want to do, it seems to me. It is a calling, and often for only one single issue or time. Sometimes I get the impression that people think serving and prophetic ministry means you talk a lot. The opposite is actually true. If you want to be reliable in prophetic ministry I believe the number two thing you can do right after learning to hear God is learning to shut up (1 Thessalonians 4:11)

Here's why you should learn to shut up if you want to be a Prophet

1. God will let you tell people's secrets.

If you operate in prophetic ministry which requires a deep strong prayer life, God will call you to pray for people and He will tell you why. That means you will know things about other people through discernment of spirits, the ability the Holy Spirit gives to discern what spirit someone is walking in or being influenced by, and through words of knowledge, where random facts come to you out of the blue because the Holy Spirit whispers them in your ear. If God tells you someone's secrets, You can be sure it is not for you to go tell people about. A better option is to tell nobody about it and pray about it first. If God wants you to bring it up to the person He will tell you to do so and will give you the opportunity to talk to the person yielding good results.

2. People will tell you their own secrets.

It is the freakiest thing, but people talk to people who hear God. The reason could vary from person to person. Maybe they do it because they know you will stand beside them in prayer. Maybe they need an encouraging word, and they know you will be able to hear what the Father is saying. Maybe they just need to vent, and they feel you are safe. Maybe they can sense the Father's love in you, and they know you will not condemn them. I hope all four of these reasons are true for every person and prophetic ministry. At any rate, people will definitely talk to you so how should you handle that? Honor their trust and keep their confidence. Protect them where possible (unless they are doing something illegal like abusing a child in which case go to the police, etc.). Speak truth to them but only as much truth as the Father releases you to speak. You'll probably have plenty that you could say from your own flesh or opinions but don't do it. If the Father doesn't tell you to say a particular thing, it is because the person is not prepared to hear it. When people tell you their secrets, you need to know how to shut up because you cannot share their secrets with others, and you can't dump all of your opinions and thoughts on them. Remember to walk in love and honor what they can handle.

3. God will tell you His own secrets!

God will give you glimpses of what He wants to do in the future. He does not do it so you can talk about it all over the place. Sometimes it is not time to release a secret like that. More often God just needs you to pray. Prayer might be the biggest reason God will tell you His secrets. When He gives you a dream, vision, word of knowledge, or prophecy about something that He wants to do, start praying like crazy! Find scriptures that support it and start speaking into those situations. If you do so, you will be a spiritual midwife, helping to birth the thing the Holy Spirit wants to release. If however, you blab about what God wants to do and He did not give you permission to talk about it somehow, can lose power.

You can lose the impetus to pray. Other people's doubt can hinder the new thing or people that aren't on the same page with what God is doing might even try to hinder it. Be very careful when God tells you about His own future plans. Pray into what He shows you, and unless He tells you to say anything, shut up.

4. **A good word at the wrong time is still the wrong thing.**

Intercessors and prophetic people tend to hear God all the time. A problem can occur, however when they think that now is always the time to share what God is has said they present a disservice to the call itself.

Here are some moments when it is probably not appropriate to share what God has said to you...

- When someone else is lost in worship and God is working them over. Please do not interrupt them unless you're the person in authority. Your word is unlikely to be more important than what God is doing.

- In the middle of a group prayer meeting, when what God told you in your quiet time that morning has nothing to do with the flow of prayer. If your word does not flow with the meeting, your word works for you, not for the group, and does not need to be shared.

- At the end of a meeting or discussion when the meeting is clearly over. You may be disappointed that you did not get a chance to share your Word, but do not worry about it. If people are done and want to leave, no one will listen anyway. Save your word for a time when people can pay attention to it. Ask God for when and where and he will give you a time to share it if it needs to be shared.

No matter where you are in learning prophetic ministry, the number one thing you can do is learn to hear God. After that, however, I firmly believe one of the most important disciplines you can develop is learning to shut up. Silence is golden when you are armed with information that could be dangerous.

Chapter 12

Where Are the Deacons?

"Likewise, must the deacons be grave, not double tongued, not given too much wine, not greedy of filthy lucre, holding the mystery of the faith in a pure conscience. And let these also first be proved, then let them use the office of a deacon, being found blameless."

1 Timothy 3:8-16

Deacons are members of the clergy along with priests and bishops. The deacon's ministry has three dimensions - liturgy, word, and service. At the liturgy, he assists the Bishop and Priest. At the mass, the Deacon proclaims the gospel, may be invited to preach the homily, and assists at the altar.

What is the role of a Deacon in the church?

What do deacons do? In short, they assist the Elders by meeting needs in the life of the church. They unleash the Word of God by allowing Elders to focus on praying, teaching and governing. In doing so, the Deacons guard and encourage the church's love for one another.

What are the qualifications of a Deacon?

(1 Timothy 3:1-13)

"Deacons, likewise, are to be men worthy of respect, sincere, not indulging in much wine, and not pursuing dishonest gain. They must keep hold of the deep truths of the faith with a clear conscience. They must first be tested, then if there is nothing against them, let them serve as deacons."

What disqualifies you from being a Deacon?

A Deacon must not be given to wine. He must not use wine unwisely in any way, nor be enslaved by it or any other food or drink that impairs his judgment. Addition to wine disqualifies a man from office. A man who becomes drunk also fails to meet this qualification for the office of Deacon in the church.

What are four responsibilities of a Deacon?

The Deacon's duties include helping members meet their temporal needs, preparing for and giving missionary service, doing family history work and being baptized for the dead, activating young men of quorum age, and learning the gospel. The quorum gives us the opportunity to work together in fulfilling these duties.

Can you be a Deacon without being ordained?

Although deacons are usually ordained for the service of ministry, there are some deacons who do not go on to receive priestly ordination, recognizing a vocation to remain in the diaconate. A permanent Deacon is also known as a "distinctive Deacon", or a "vocational Deacon." Most potential clerics always more than likely skip this process of elevation, which is that of a Deacon. In doing so most will aim for the higher call or title within the church.

This is not an accomplishment but a misfortune and leaves room for misdiagnosis within the church. We as clergy should never believe that we are higher than those who serve; as a matter of fact it is in Zachariah's account (Zechariah 4:10), "despise not small beginnings." Everyone should be a Deacon at heart, whether you are part of the fivefold or Bishop in the Lord's church. Remember this one mere fact, Deacons are called to serve the church and take care of their ministry needs. Deacons, basically put, are ministers of the people, and a key part of the care ministries of the church. Deacons unify people. Acts 6:1-7 is a great example of how seven leaders can promote unity by taking care of the needs of the church.

The ministry to which a person is called when he or she becomes a Deacon or Deaconess include the following duties:

1. Greeting and Ushering

2. Upkeep of the church property

3. Security

4. Visitation

5. Assisting with baptismal ceremonies

6. Assisting with the communion service

7. Caring for the congregation

Leading Worship

Deacons are fully authorized to lead worship, preach, conduct funerals, and preside over weddings (provided that they register with their state or county office to receive state authorization to officiate state recognized marriages.)

They often work together with elders, and when doing so, it is traditional for the deacons to handle these portions of worship.

- Reading the gospel lesson
- leading the prayers of concern for the world, the church, and the needy
- leading the Lord's prayer
- receiving the offering
- dismissing the people to service before the elder offers the benediction

Deacons also trained laypeople to lead portions of the worship service and are called to assist elders in the sacraments of Holy Communion and baptism. In rare instances, a Bishop may authorize a Deacon to preside at the sacraments in the absence of an elder.

Keep in mind, the name Deacon (diakonos), means only "minister" or "servant", and is employed in this sense both in the Septugant (though only in the book of Esther, e.g. 2:2, 6:3) and in the New Testament (e.g. Matthew 20:28, Romans 15:25, Ephesians 3.7, etc.) But in Apostolic times the word began to acquire a more definite and technical meaning writing around 63 AD. Saint Paul addresses, "all the Saints who are at Philippi with the bishops and deacons," (Phillipians 1:1). A few years later, as referenced in 1Timothy 3:8, He impresses upon Timothy that, "deacons must be chaste, not double tongued, not given too much wine, not greedy for filthy lucre, holding the mystery of faith in a pure conscious." He directs further that they must, "first be proved, and so let them minister, having no crime." He adds that they should be the husband of one wife, who rule their children well in their own houses."

This passage is worthy of noting, not only because it describes the qualities desirable in candidates for the diaconate, but also because it's just the sternal administration and the handling of money we're likely to form a part of their functions. Remember in Acts 6, Stephen is an essential character and the forerunner of Deacon. The narratives of Acts 6:1-6, which serves to introduce the account of the martyrdom of Stephen, describes the first institution of the office of Deacon. The Apostles, in order to meet the complaints of the Hellenistic Jews that "their widows were neglected in the daily ministrations" (diakonia), called together the multitude of the disciples and said,

"It is not reason that we should leave the word of God and serve (diakonen) tables. Wherefore, brethren, look ye out seven men of good reputation, full of the Holy Ghost and wisdom, whom we may appoint over this business. But we will give ourselves continuously to prayer and to the ministry of the word (the "diakoniatou loguou".) And the saying was liked by all the multitude. And they chose Stephen a man full of faith and of the Holy Ghost."

Now, on the ground that the seven are not expressly called Deacons and that some of them (e.g. St. Stephen and later Phillpi (Acts 21:8), preached and right next to the Apostles, Protestant commentators having constantly raised objections against the identification of this choice of the seven with the institution of the diaconate. But apart from the fact that the tradition among the fathers is both unanimous and early, e.g. St. Irenaeus (Adv. Haer, III, XII, IO and IV, XV, 1) speaks of St. Stephen is the first Deacon, the similarity between the functions of the seven who served the tables and those of the early deacons is most striking. Compare, for example, both with the passage from Acts with 1 Timothy 3:8. Remember, deacons serve and so should we, that is all a part of the clergy.

Chapter 13

Dressed for the Wrong Occasion

In this chapter I would like to deal with the cleric attire. It irritates me as a Bishop in the Lord's church to see clergy in the wrong attire. Misdiagnosed in the church - it is a pet peeve of mine and I would like to address this topic here.

There are situations in which clothing is very important. Clothing conveys a message. A business suit says, "money!" A police uniform says, "law." A tuxedo says, "wedding." Casual clothing says, "me!" Clericals say, "church!" Any of those messages might be valid in different contexts, so you have to make sure you are wearing the right clothes for the occasion. If you wear a business suit in a department store, people will mistake you for the manager. If you were to go to a ball game, they will not ask you to play. If you wear a jogging suit to a fancy restaurant, your clothing says, "I wandered in here by mistake," and the staff will treat you accordingly. The word clericals refer to the "special clothing that clergy wear outside of worship services", usually consisting of a white collar on a black shirt (for male clergy) or on a black blouse (for female clergy), combined with other clothing that is either black or grey.

If you are a Pastor and you think you are aggrandizing yourself when you wear clericals, you will be disappointed. The congregation quickly gets used to the clericals and they see them as badge of service, not honor. Clericals put you in the same functional category as bellhops, waiters, police officers, airline pilots, and so on. We do not dress to please ourselves or anyone else for that matter - our manner of dress facilitates our service. It makes our function obvious to strangers. It makes our duties inescapable, and it constrains our personal conduct, because we cannot disappear into the crowd when we are wearing our clericals. Clericals mean that visitors don't have to ask, "where is the Pastor?" They know just by looking.

What is the Priest wearing?

Interestingly, you would think that the priestly vestments of today would find their origins in the ceremonial dress that is described in the Old Testament. For instance, in Exodus 28:2-4, we read:

"For the glorious adornment of your brother Aaron you shall have sacred vestments made. Therefore, tell the various artisans whom I have endowed with the skill to make vestments for Aaron to consecrate him as my priest. These are the vestments they shall make: a breastpiece, an ephod, a robe, a brocade tunic, a turban, and a sash."

Instead, the beginning of the holy vestments of the Christian Church came from the everyday garb of the Greco-Roman world. At the heart of this 1st century dress was the tunic and the mantle. The Greeks believed that the tunic, draped from the shoulder, was symbolic of the body and its movements. They believed that this enveloping cloak around the body with the head in the center expressed the spiritual and intellectual profession of men. In the Roman world during the 2nd century, the dalmatic, which was a loose and belted tunic with very wide sleeves came about; it was the outer garment worn over the long white tunic. Interestingly, it was stripped and for the most part is the outer garment still worn today.

By the 4th century, garments worn at liturgical functions have been separated from those of everyday life. Priests could be distinguished by certain ornamentation add it to the everyday dress. It was also at this time that the stole began to be used as official symbols of holy priesthood. The first mention of a special liturgical garment for sacred worship comes from Theodore+ of Cyrus (d.c. 457.) In his writing on church history, he noted that in 330 AD, emperor Constantine presented to the new church in Jerusalem a sacred robe which was to be used by the Bishop at baptisms and Easter vigil. Documents during this time also reflected the fact that many were divided on the question of special liturgical vestments. For instance, the early Christian author Tertullian reject it special dress while Clement of Alexandria

95

advocated it. Pope Clement I, during his pontificate Century noted, "Bishops should be distinguished from the people costume but not doctrine."

By the ninth century, the plain vestments of old tended to be more and more elaborately decorated. It was here when Pontifical gloves appeared. The mitre or ceremonial headdress most commonly seen on the heads of Bishops came about in the tenth century. Liturgical shoes and stockings worn by Bishops and Cardinals appeared in the eleventh century. Today the draping form of the vestments such as the alb, the dalmatic and the chasuble puts the emphasis on his liturgical role. As such, the priest body is "hidden" in a way that takes him away as the center of the liturgical action and recognizes the true source and summit of the celebration, Jesus Christ. The priest thus wears the vestments not in his own name but rather in "persona Christi."

Liturgical colors

> **"It starts with purple and ends with green, and there is a white and red in between."**

What do the different colors used by the Priests signify? As outlined by the church different colors have been green, white, purple, red and black.

Green signifies "ordinary time in the church." It must be noted that the shades of green can vary. For instance, the grain of spring is a different shade than that of November as the church year ends.

Purple is worn during Advent and Lent. Similar to purple, is the color rose which is worn just two Sundays throughout the year. First is the third Sunday of advent, otherwise known as Gaudete Sunday. During lent, it is worn during the fourth Sunday, also known a Laetare Sunday.

> **White denotes time of great celebration as seen in the Christmas and Easter seasons.**

White vestments are also worn at baptisms, weddings, ordinations and feast days of the Lord, The blessed mother and Saints who were not martyrs. Red implies the blood of Christ. It is put on by the priest on Pentecost and for confirmations. Black, rarely seen, can be worn during the office of the dead. It may also be worn on Good Friday.

Garments today

- Amice — A rectangular neck cloth which serves to protect the valuable chasuble and stole but is used only if the alb does not cover the ordinary clothing at the neck.

- Alb - A long, white garment worn by the priest to represent the new and Immaculate vestment that has been received through baptism.

- Stole - A long narrow band, several inches wide and about 80 inches long (and the same color as the chasuble) which is worn as a sign that the Priest is serving and his official liturgical role.

- Cinture - A cord used as a belt to tighten the alb symbolizing the virtue of chastity and continence and is the same color as the chasuble.

- Chasuble - the final vestment of the priest that is worn over all the others and symbolizes the virtue of charity and the yoke of unselfish love.

- Cassock - Long garment worn by clergy both as ordinary dress and under liturgical garments. The cassock, with button closure, has long sleeves and fits the body closely.

The color and trim vary with the ecclesiastical ranking of the wearer. The Pope wears plain white and Cardinals, black with scarlet trim. Archbishops and Bishops wear black with red trim and lesser clergy, plain black.

- Cope - liturgical vestment worn by clergy and some Angelica and clergy at non-eucharistic functions. It is a full-length cloak usually made of silk or other rich material in various colors formed from a semicircular piece of cloth with a hood attached to the neck. Unlike the similar chasuble, the cope is open at the front and is fastened at the breast by hooks or brooch. The cope can be worn by all ranks of the clergy and is used in almost all functions in which the chasuble is not worn, such as dorm processions blessings and burials.

Dress for the wrong occasion

In liturgical rites, clerics shall wear the vesture prescribed in the proper liturgical books. Outside liturgical functions will consist of a black suit, a collar and the usual attire for clergy.

What do different colors of clergy shirts mean?

Members of the clergy wear black shirts as their predominant color. Members of the clergy who occupy the rank of Bishop are usually awarded a Crimson or maroon shirt. Apostles are also awarded a red shirt.

Blue Clergy Wear – Prophets and Overseers

Grey Clergy Wear - Deacons

Proper clergy attire

The word "clericals" refer to the special clothing that clergy wear outside of worship services, usually consisting of a white collar on a black shirt for male clergy or on a black blouse for female clergy.

What is Class A clergy attire?

The robe is usually made from a heavy fabric and features a high collar and long sleeves. The stole is a long, narrow piece of fabric that is draped around the neck and shoulders and is often decorated with embroidery or other embellishments.

As I conclude this chapter, please be reminded that proper clergy wear should always be implemented. Dress according to the occasion.

Chapter 14

The Gift of Apostle

"Am I Called"

One of the questions many will ask is they learn that God is calling forth Apostles in this hour is "am I one of them?" Deep within each of us is a desire to be used effectively by God. The Apostolic call is going forth, summoning some to become Apostolic people, others to become Apostles, and we must discern between the two. How does a person know if he or she is called beyond the role of an Apostolic person to actually become an Apostle??

The life of the Apostle Paul becomes a picture of the Apostle-level apostolic calling in action. Four progressive stages are involved in calling an Apostle and in the person's awareness of that calling.

1. The intuition of a call.

The initial stage of a personal Apostolic call for Paul came to him intuitively. He knew that God was calling him as an Apostle because God had shown it to him personally (see Galatians 1:15). For any Apostle in the making, the Apostolic call begins as an inner knowledge of a spiritual sense that is clearly from God. This is just the beginning of a progressive outworking of the Apostolic calling.

2. The intimidation of a call.

The next level of the personal calling Paul experience came as an implication from Ananias just after Paul met Christ (see Acts 9:10-19.) Jesus had told Ananias while he was in prayer that Paul was a chosen vessel. When Ananias prayed for Paul, he was filled with the Spirit. Ananias shared his message from God with Paul, and though apostleship was not specifically mentioned Paul's understanding that God was calling him was confirmed through another. Outside confirmation is an important key in the process of identifying and substantiating the Apostolic call. Clearly Paul accepted the call and began to pursue it from that day.

3. The indication of a call.

As time went on, the intuition and intimidation of the call progressed to a clear prophetic sanction. The best scriptural pattern we have for the process of selecting, ordaining and setting legitimate Apostles into office is the account of the prophetic gathering at Antioch. As the Apostles prayed at Antioch, Paul and Barnabas were singled out by the voice of God as chosen instruments (see Acts 13:2). This tells us that the appointment of the Apostle is a spirit led activity that is done publicly and in a context of prayer and worship and that several proven leaders need to agree, make no mistake about it. To proceed in apostolic ministry without the keys of a prophetic, public, and plural ordination by proven ministries would be entirely out of order in the emerging Apostolic movement. Each candidate for the apostolic ministry must wait upon this kind of experience before pursuing the fullness of an apostolic call. In this way, many abuses and errors can be avoided. The apostolic network I am involved in uses this as the working pattern to guide us safely through the process of ordaining apostles.

4. The impartation of a call.

The final confirmation of an apostolic calling came to Paul as hands were laid upon him in that same corporate gathering (see Acts 13:3.) Upon hearing what the spirit of God was saying, God used the brethren at Antioch to impart blessings and anointing to Paul and Barnabas. Laying on of hands imparted divine power into the lives of these Apostles and was the final seal upon their calling. Each person God calls to participate in the emerging Apostolic movement, whether called as an Apostle or simply as an apostolic person, needs to discern the nature of a personal calling, and respond accordingly. The calling will come intuitively and will ultimately progress to an impartation of supernatural power. Now it is necessary for us to be alert and responsive to the apostolic call. At Pentecost a sound came from heaven with the outpouring (Acts 2:2). Our ears must be open to the heavenly sound of our day period from beyond the realm of business as usual to each of us Jesus says, "follow Me." He is echoing the Father's heart. He is walking the shorelines of our lives interrupting our activity and calling all of us to drop our nets in one dimension or another. When we do, we undergo radical changes and become apostolic people.

The Twelve Apostles of the Lamb

Included in this company are the twelve Apostles. "Then he appointed twelve, that they might be with Him and that He might send them out to preach, "to have power to heal sickness and to cast out demons." (Mark 3:14-15). Jesus chose the twelve Apostles early in His earthly ministry. Christ conferred upon them the title of Apostle (See Luke 6:13). The twelve apostles included Peter, James, John, Andrew, Phillip, Nathaniel, Thomas, Matthew, James the son of Alpheus, Simon, Thaddeus and Judas who was replaced by Matthias. Christ shared His ministry with these twelve men. They are distinguished by several unique factors. Each of the twelve Apostles of the lamb personally witnessed the resurrection and ascension of Jesus (see Acts 1:9, 22, 2:32, 3:15, 4:33, 5:30-32, 10:39-42). No one knew Christ more fully than they and none have since been personally trained by Christ on earth. Because they worked and lived directly with Jesus, they shall remain preeminent among the entire apostolic company, and will possess a special prominence in the kingdom that that other New Testament Apostles will not achieve (see Matthew 19:28, Rev 21: 14).

Other New Testament Apostles

It is clear that there were more apostles than the twelve Apostles of the Lamb. These are referred to as secondary Apostles by some theologians because they are designated in scripture as Apostles but some do not have the unique prominence and the kingdom that the original twelve had. These Apostles include some of the greatest world changers in history and this kind of Apostle continues on today as the normative kind.

The New Testament mentions the following names as those who were secondary Apostles : Matthias (Acts 1:26), Paul (1 Cor 15:8), James, The brother of Jesus (Galatians 1:19), Barnabas (Acts 14:3, 4, 14), Apollos (1 Cor. 4:6-9), Timothy (Acts 19:22, 1 Thess. 1:1, 2:6), Titus (2 Cor. 8:23, where "messenger" as Apostolos), Silas or Silvanus (Acts 15:22, 1 Thess. 1:1, 2:6), Tychicus (2 Tim. 4:12), Judas (Acts 15:22; 1 Thess. 2:6), Andronicus (Romans 16:7), Junia, whose name indicates this might have been a woman (Romans 16:7), Epaphroditus (Phil

2:25), Erastus (Acts 19:22) and two unnamed Apostles (2 Cor. 8:23.) If the twelve Apostles are added to this list a total of thirty-two Apostles would be mentioned in the New Testament. All of these were sent by God as valid Apostolic ministers and members of the Apostolic company of the New Testament.

The 70

"After these things the Lord appointed seventy others, also, and sent them two by two before his face into every city and place where he himself was about to go."

Luke 10:1

This broader body of disciples was sent by Christ and went everywhere preaching and ministering healing and deliverance. The number seventy was special and symbolic in israel. Seventy elders were present with Moses in the wilderness (see Numbers 11:16-25), and they became symbolic of the spirit of Christ coming on his people. Seventy was the number of the nations of the earth as found in Genesis 10; this number is a symbol of the whole earth to which the seventy were sent. Some writers maintained that the next generation of Apostles were selected from among the seventy disciples.

The seventy disciples are included of the apostolic company because they were the original apostolic people that is, people who were sent and appointed by Christ for active ministry. Though they were not Apostles, they did apostolic works healing the sick preaching the gospel, reestablishing the work of god as apostolic people. They all operated under the same apostolic mandate of Christ. In today's churches it seems as if everyone that is up for evaluation wants to be an Apostle. Most of the ones who want to operate as an Apostle is in most cases, not a true Apostle. I will go on to say further that these newly appointed Apostles are pretty much misdiagnosed in the church, operating as such with no evidence for being one. Even God Himself expressed in Revelation 2:2,

"I know your works, your labor, your patience, and that you cannot bear those who are evil period and you have tested those who say they are apostles and are not, and have found them liars."

Responding to the Apostolic call

In many ways, the church has been slow to walk in these truths, not properly understanding the full extent and reach of the Apostolic call. From the pre–Incarnate Christ and through the first-century Apostles throughout the generations, to our present day, the call is echoing.

The Apostles must come forth! Why have we explained most of it away? Have we been idle assuming that the apostolic call was only temporary in the church? Paul clearly says that Apostles will function until the Body of Christ is fully matured (See Ephesians 4:11-13.) Others have maintained that even if apostles do exist, they are expected to bear the weight of all apostolic work period their reasoning has been, let Evangelists do the evangelizing. Let the Apostles do the Apostolic work. But nothing could be further from the intention of the father. No wonder real apostolic results have been scarce! It is as though we have obeyed a "Great Omission, "instead of the 'Great Commission.'" We must acknowledge that the entire body of Christ is responsible for carrying out the apostolic vision of the Father at some level. None are excluded from the vineyard, though not all are Apostles, "for many are called." (Matthew 20:16)

Chapter 15

The Bishopric

Let's talk about the bishopric. This is the final chapter of the book, and I purposely left the Bishopric last for a reason, being that I myself am a Bishop in the Lord's church.

I was ordained and consecrated as a Bishop in the early part of 2016. I remember the morning of my elevation so vividly. I knew prior to my elevation that my work in the kingdom aligned with the Bishopric. Not only was I an established Pastor, and married to a wonderful woman, who happened to be an apostle in the Lord's church, but I also had begun to father and pastor many spiritual sons and daughters. I had learned so much over the years that I had grasped hold to the bishopric. I have learned ancient faith and also the sacraments of the ancient church. Being a Bishop is a vocation that allows one to work in excellency and become one who can serve rather than be served. It is in this final chapter of this book that I will introduce the bishopric to you.

First and foremost, what is a Bishop?

A Bishop is a senior member of the Christian clergy, usually in charge of a diocese and empowered to confer holy orders. A Bishop is someone having spiritual or ecclesiastical supervision over others. Also, a Bishop is an ordained member of the clergy who is entrusted with a position of authority and oversight in a religious institution. In Christianity Bishops are normally responsible for the governance and administration of diocese. The role or office of the Bishop is called episcopacy.

What are the three main roles of the Bishop in the church?
A Bishop has the power to make church laws, be a judge in church matters and to enforce observance of these laws. These laws generally relate to worship, preaching, administration of the sacraments, safeguarding the faith and morals of the faithful and religious instruction.

What does it mean to be a Bishop in the Bible?
The word originally signified as "Overseer," or "spiritual superintendent." The title Bishop and Elder or Presbyters were essentially equivalent. Bishop is from the Greek and denotes one who exercises the function of overseeing.

Bishops are Ordained.

Ordination is the sacramental ceremony in which a man or woman becomes a Deacon, Priest, or Bishop and enabled to minister in Christ's name and that of the church. There are three ordinations in the sacrament of holy orders — diaronate, priesthood and episcopal.

Let's Dig into the Bishopric

Every Bishop has within them an apostolate. (The work of the apostles during the 1st century patriotic, has been passed to the Bishops to continue within their churches, diocese and communities they serve.) The Bishops have, by divine institution, taking the place of the Apostles as Pastors of the church. The Bishops received the charge of the community presiding in God's steed over the flock of which they are shepherds and that they are teachers of doctrine, ministers of sacred worship and holders of the office and government. The Bishop, as vicars and the gates of Christ, govern the particular churches assigned to them. In virtue of this power, Bishops have a sacred right and duty before the Lord of legislating.

The Bishop is chosen one of two ways:

1. Appointed

Bishop-Designate is the title prior to consecration. They must be appointed by one higher than themselves. A bishop cannot make himself a bishop.

2. Elected

Bishop-Elect is the title prior to consecration. Various clergy and bishops who desire one to be the Bishop over them, he lets them, and requests a consecration.

A Bishop's Responsibilities

- Must have a clear sense of the purpose and mission of the church.

- Must have several years of experience as an ordained cleric: Apostle, Pastor, Teacher, Prophet, Evangelist

- Has been trained as a Presbyter and has experienced shepherding

- Background in his teaching and preaching

- Should have a criminal background check

- Is conscious of the community

- Is a spiritual and government leader

- Judges all matters relating to the local church, and those under his or her jurisdiction.

- Should be installed and consecrated into the office.

- Is an overseer at large.

- Clergy of the highest order is charged with supervision or an administrative function

Ethics for the Office of the Bishop

- First and foremost, must grasp every opportunity to hear from God

- Must keep mind in perfect peace

- Is the greatest servant among the servants

- Those around the Bishop must guard and protect his name

- Has spiritual persona

- Teachers with authority

- Must fashion themselves to walk after the church

- Makes appointments, licenses, ordains, diaconate, elders and consecrates other bishops

- Must keep a balance- leadership vs. friendship (maintain boundaries)

- Develop his or her spouse (if we don't take care of our wives, we will not take care of the church.

Just a Few Levels of the Episcopacy

I will not name all of the levels, but I will address at least six of them.

1. **Primate**: a presiding Bishop. Color is signified by scarlet red.

2. **Prelate**: a successor to primate, those who give final word, head of a territory or jurisdiction of a diocese.

3. **Coadjutor**: and administrative office, assistance to prelate. Immediate successor to prelate. Cannot do anything without the Prelate's authorization.

4. **Suffragen:** Assistant to the primate. Has no direct succeeding line. Cannot ordain. Administrative secretary.
5. **Auxiliary:** leader over department heads (no territory)
6. **Titulas:** Bishop Emeritus - no portfolio of charges. Retired from active service but retains one's title.

The Attire of the Episcopacy

Roman purple - church color with gold chain and cross

Black shirt - corporate attire

Travel - corporate black

Scarlet Red - only for the primate

(never wear scarlet red in the presence of a primate)

Civic - black shirt with a collar

Proper Episcopal Dress

Class A	Class B	Class C
Cassock	Cassock	Cassock
Cincture	Cincture (Fuchsia)	Cincture (Fuchsia)
Surplice	Rochet	Surplice
Mozzetta	Chimere	Manteletta
Cordone w/ cross	Pastoral Cross/Chain	Cordone w/ cross
Zucchetto	Chain	Zucchetto
Biretta	Tippet (A stole may be used in place of tippet.)	Biretta

Choir dress is the traditional vesture of the clerics, seminarians, and religious of Christian churches worn for public prayer and the administration of the sacraments except when celebrating or celebrating the Eucharist originated in the sixteenth century. Choir dress also differs from house dress which is worn outside of the liturgical context (whether in the house or on the street.) House dress may be formal or informal.

Mass Cassock – has a removable shoulder cape. A house cassock shoulder cape is attached.

Priests (Elders and Presbyters) and bishops have different clergy attire. Choir dress is ceremonial and functional for church business and is regarded as Class B.

What does choir attire consist of?

Standard choir attire for seminarians, deacons, and priests consists of the following:

1. black cassock (soutane, sarum)
2. cincture
3. surplice
4. stole or tippet (for ordained orders) / (Anglican choir attire / academic choir)

The surplice is a loose white vestment varying from hip length to calf length, worn over a cassock by clergy, acolytes, and choristers at Christian church services. Those who have been admitted into Holy Orders view the surplus as the priestly garment signifying the purless of the priesthood of Christ.

Proper Cassock Colors

The Cassock - a long, black garment worn under everything else.

Surplice - a long, but not so long vestment with full sleeves. The history is interesting: (The name comes from the Latin meaning "garment" worn over furs.)

Stole – a long scarf of fabric matching. It symbolizes in ordination representing the yoke of Christ. (The black tippet is equivalent to the stole.)

Alb - an all-white, ankle length vestment with long sleeves. The stall is worn over the alb, at the waist with a cincture (latin word is "girdle.)

Chasuble - (from the latin word "little house) is a vestment made out of silk, and is oval, large and sleeveless with an opening in the center for the Priest's head. This garment is worn when conducting the Eucharist (Holy Communion).

Bishop Mitre (Distinguishing marks of the Episcopate): Tall, double pointed hat - Old and New Testament, it origins as far back as the oriental era; it came to the ecclesiastical order around year 1100.

Chemere - sleeveless garment worn formally as a part of academic dress.

Rochet - A vestment resembling a surplus, used chiefly by bishops.

FYI
For Your Information

It takes at least three years for a novice to become an Episcopate to be ranked because elder Episcopal college members precede them in preference, performance, and trust. We need to understand the classical meaning of titles, styles, and honors instead of using them not knowing and making ourselves appear confused and incompetent.

Additional notes for your consideration...

Fourth century Episcopal vestments are liturgical vestments, ceremonial vestments and sacramental vestments.

Ecclesiastical vestments:

choir dress - warned during convocations and worn by other prelates, bishops, or superior ranks.

Prelate – pronounced (Prell-eht) not (Pre-late)

a prelate is a high-ranking member of the Christian clergy who is an ordinary (ruling a diocese.) The word derives from the Latin "Praelatus" the past principle of "praeferre", which means "carry before," or prefer, hence a prelate is one set over others.

Installation

To install is to be installed into a stall such as in a cathedral. The word itself literally means, "to place in a stall." Remember, ordination can always be revoked. The first defrocking was commanded by God which is where we get the word "defrock" from, which means to remove the vestments. Defrocking can be done for various reasons. Your ordination does not automatically transfer from church to church without being properly released from your former church, reformation, or denomination. It is always up to the receiving church to reject or accept your orders.

Chapter 16
Vocabulary

Most people that have been elevated too soon, will show it in their vocabulary. I believe one should be well versed, when it comes to vocabulary and when it comes to episcopal lingo. In this final bonus chapter, I will give some examples on how to greet a Bishop; I will also give vocabulary and its definitions, so that one may be just a little more verse, when entertaining others in the clergy field. No more being listed as "misdiagnosed", it is my prayer that after this tutorial chapter one will never again be labeled as "misdiagnosed in the church."

Five-Fold Ministry:

Where did the term fivefold ministry come from? Is it a biblical term or is it an apostolic term? Was it a development or was it ancient? The history about the fivefold doctrine teaching is demonstrated with the hand.

1. Apostle – thumb

2. Prophet – index finger

3. Evangelist – third finger

4. Shepherds – ring finger

5. Teachers – pinky finger

In 1824, the term fivefold ministry came about, created by a man named Edward Irving, a Presbyterian pastor in Scotland. Edward Irving is one who believed in the movement of the Holy Ghost, in which he did not see at the Presbyterian Church. Today, we are more caught up in giftings than the orthodoxy.

Orthodoxy Is defined as "authorized or generally accepted theory, doctrine, or practice." It comes from the Greek words "orthos" which means "right, true or straight," and "doxa" meaning "opinion." So, orthodoxy describes the one true opinion. The noun orthodoxy pronounced, "or-thuh-dock-see", is the most commonly used to talk about religious beliefs.

Bishop – "one that governs":

A senior member of the Christian clergy usually in charge of a diocese and empowered to confer orders. A Bishop is an ordained member of the clergy who is entrusted with a position of authority and oversight in a religious institution. Bishops are normally responsible for the governance and administration of the diocese.

Apostle: "one who is sent"

Apostles are not supposed to govern. Some apostles believe that only an apostle can affirm another Apostle. This is biblical manipulation, Being that it is nowhere in scripture. If we look at Acts 13, we find that the Apostle Paul was not affirmed by another Apostle he was confirmed by a Bishop, Lucius, by a Prophet and a Teacher in this case, known as leadership. I'm going further-according to the rule of consecration you need a total of three to make a Bishop.

Rite: A religious or other solemn ceremony or act.

You have heard of the Roman rite, the Syrian rite, the Angelical rite, Abyssian right, etc. (The Abyssian Rite is also known as the Ethiopian Rite.)

Rights are the family of religious services, observances and rituals performed within a particular church. It must have a scriptural basis, a purpose for performing it and a ceremony to exercise it publicly. Typically, a rite from within the liturgical church has styles that address formal and celebratory high church services. Usually, the Priest or Bishop serves the eucharist with their back to the audience (adorientem) on a raised table. Low church, which has a more charismatic focus, extemporaneous praise, prayers and a Pentecostal field with a bare minimum of litany, readings, collects and the like. If there is a eucharist celebration, the priest or bishop serves facing the congregation (verses poplum).

Broad church - best for ecumenical services where there are expressions from various Christian denominations, philosophies and perspectives.

What is the difference between a presiding Bishop, prelate, patriarch or metropolitan?

First and foremost, all five of these roles are not offices within themselves, but designations of persons who are in the office of the Bishop. I want to start with an understanding of the roles specifically for an Archbishop; that is Primate, or Primacy. The title of the Primate is bestowed upon certain archbishops and specific Christian rites or traditions. Depending on the tradition or rite, it can signify either jurisdictional authority (a title of authority), or more commonly, ceremonial precedence (a title of honor, usually awarded to senior Archiepiscopates.)

The Latin Church of Primate is typically an Archbishop (and occasionally a suffragan or exempt Bishop) of a specific primatial. The primate has precedence over the bishoprics of one or more ecclesiastical provinces within a particular historical, political, or cultural area. The primate may be serving as presiding over in ecclesiastical House of bishops within the diocese or archdiocese.

Historically, primates enjoyed privileges (prelature) such as presiding over national synods, hearing appeals from metropolitan tribunals, crowding the nation sovereign, and conducting the investor of the archbishops. However, in modern times, especially in the United States among Pentecostals, charismatic Baptists and others, the office is largely honorific and holds no effective sacerdotal or ecclesiastic powers because of the absence of these church practices of Canon law or sacramental worship, true diocesen structures.

Vocabulary Time

Investiture - placing of authority

Vesting - placing of any clothing

Vestment - liturgical, not choir dress

Concave - a secret, private meeting

(con – "meeting" / clavis – "with a key")

Sigillum - from signet ring

Canon - an ecclesiastical rule or law

Polity - a form or process of civil government or constitution

What is a Synod?

A Synod is a gathering (regional or church wide) of Apostles and Bishops to resolve a church crisis. The Apostles convened for the first cyanide, or council of the church and about 50 AD (see Acts 15). The first crisis of the church took place when Christianity was not even two decades old. There had already been disagreements and even controversies, but this crisis was an issue that got to the very heart of the definition of Christianity itself.

More vocabulary

Anglican - a member of one of the churches descended from the Church of England

Acolyte - a person, usually but not always a youth, and a simple white vestment who lights the altar candles.

Diaconate - the office of Deacon

Rector - a full-time priest elected by a vestry with the Bishop's approval

Postuiant - a person admitted by the Bishop into the formal preparation for ordained ministry

Offertory - the offering of bread and wine

Sub Deacon - assistant to the diocesan deacons

Presbyter – Greek word (Presbuteros), "the term priest"

Vestry - the official representations of the parish

Apostolic Succession

The doctrine that the authority and the mission given by Jesus to the Apostles have descended in a direct and unbroken line of bishops to the Bishops today.

More Vocabulary

Ecclesiology - study of the church

Catholic - Greek word "katholikes" which means "universal" church.

Kataholos:

Kata - according to

Holos - whole, complete

Kath'olou – translates to "Catholic"

"Catholic" is noted in the bible as found in Acts 9:31. When someone sees the word Catholic, they immediately go to Italy, Rome, Pope, Vatican, etc. (worshiping Mary and Saints). Rome is not a church, it is an empire (380 AD.)

Acts 9:31 - The church (Catholic) enjoys the time of peace. Remember, Catholic refers to the "Universal Church."

More Vocabulary

Excardination - when one leaves and renounces their former authority and all that came with it, including credentials, assignments, and appointments. (They leave with nothing.)

Incardination -all that was left is evaluated, and the new church chooses to receive them at whatever level they decide. The church issues new assignments, new documents, and new papers. This usually happens at the same rank they left with.

Theology:
Theo – "God"
Logy – "Study of"
Theology Is not a bad word; it is a compound word. When we combine these two parts we get the word theology, the study of god. The scriptures tell us to follow on to know the Lord; Paul says, "that I may know Him."

Ambassador - general, set man, life coach, shepherd mother

Miasma - to stain or pollute

Salutiferous - conductive to health

Adytum - sacred part of a temple or church

Logorrhea - and excessive flow of words

Theologaster - petty or shallow theologian

Morosophy - foolish pretense of wisdom

Psychomachy - conflict between the body and the soul

Lecter - lay minister

Collegialism - theory that church is independent from the state

Curate - a member of the clergy serving as assistant

Misosophy - hatred of knowledge or wisdom

Formation - maturity and humanities, academics, service intellectual development

Why are bishops called "his grace"?

As for the titles "His grace," and "His Holiness," it means the grace on God bestowed not of their personal worth, but of their role in the church.

Right Reverend - a title given to a Bishop

Most Reverend - an honorific style gives in to certain high-ranking religious figures

His Grace - when speaking to an Archbishop

His Eminence- when speaking to a cardinal

* both Archbishop and Bishop would be greeted as "your excellency."

One final thought

I trust that you have enjoyed this book. As you move forward I wish you success and suggest that you keep in mind:

1. **Everything begins with a thought. "Life consists of what a man is thinking about all day."** – Ralph Waldo Emerson
2. What we think determines who we are. Who we are determines what we do. **"The actions of men are**

the best interpreters of their thoughts." – John Locke

3. Our thoughts determine our destiny. Our destiny determines our legacy. **"You are today where your thoughts have brought you. You will be tomorrow where your thoughts take you."** -James Allen

4. People who go to the top think differently than others. **"Nothing limits achievements like small thinking; nothing is man's possibilities like unleashed thinking."** – William Authur Ward

5. We can change the way we think. **"Whatever things are true, noble, just, pure, lovely and of good report. If there be any virtue and if there is anything praiseworthy think on these things."** – Paul the Apostle

A Dedication to those who helped me to become....

"For just as the body is one and has many members, and all the members of the body, though many, are one body, so it is with Christ. 13 For in one Spirit we were all baptized into one body—Jews or Greeks, slaves[a] or free—and all were made to drink of one Spirit. 14 For the body does not consist of one member but of many."

1 Corinthians 12:12-14

You are where it all began.
Thank you for loving me, protecting me and being
the best mother a man could have ever asked for.
I love you!

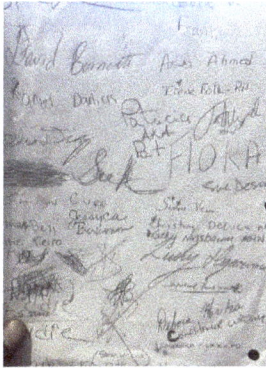

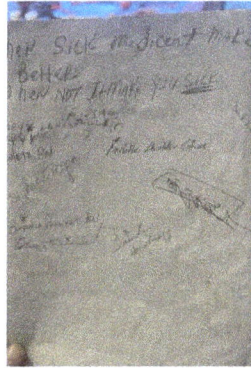

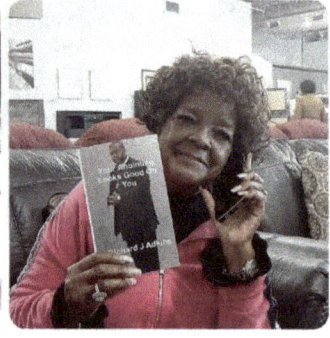

"Our goal as parents
should be to
endeavor to pass
down our faith to the
next generation in
such a way that they
will be able to pass
down their faith to
the following
generation in our
absence."
-Unknown

"We cannot live only for ourselves. A thousand fibers
connect us with our fellow men."
- Herman Melville

"The greatness of a community is most accurately measured by the compassionate actions of its members."
- Coretta Scott King

"There is one body [of believers] and one Spirit—just as you were called to one hope when called [to salvation]."
Ephesians 4:4

Notes

1. Jerry Drace, evangelistic association
2. www.openthebible.org
3. Laura J. Davis
4. Prodigal Press
5. David Cannistraci
6. www.wikipedia.org
7. John C. Maxwell , How Successful People Think
8. www.simplycatholic.com
9. Bishop E. L. Warren
10. Thirst (https://thirst.sg)
11. www.eldersdigest.org
12. Mirriam Webster
13. Irenaeus, "Adv.Haer"
14. Bishop David J. Davis, B.Th, M.Div, STM, DD
15. Edward Irving
16. Oxford Languages

Connect with the Author
Bishop Richard J. Adkins

Richard J Adkins was born January 20, 1970 in Brooklyn, NY to the parents of Richard Adkins, Sr. and Charlotte Braswell. Richard attended Sullivan County college where he studied communications. In 2005 the Lord called and chose Richard Adkins out of darkness into the marvelous light to begin his royal priesthood in Christ Jesus.

He was fully licensed and ordained by the late Apostle Brown who installed him as a minister for the people of God. Diligently working in the ministerial vineyard, the Lord Jesus Christ elevated Richard from minister to elder to pastoral Elder to Pastor within a ten-year span. Shortly afterward Richard was affirmed an Apostle in the Lord's church in 2015 and consecrated as a Bishop in 2016. Richard shares his ministry with his wife, Apostle Shaun Adkins as they both serve as the lead establishers of Impact/Redzone City of refuge Church in Greensboro, North Carolina. Richard is happily married now for more than a decade; they share 11 children in total with seven grandchildren. Richard released his first book entitled, "your anointing looks good on you," in 2014. His second installment, "misdiagnosed in the church, is being released in the summer of 2024 with additional literary works to come!

His spiritual parents are both known in the states as well as internationally – Bishop George Bloomer serving as his spiritual father and Apostle Janice Thomas, his spiritual mother.

www.ingramcontent.com/pod-product-compliance
Lightning Source LLC
Chambersburg PA
CBHW070813100426
42742CB00012B/2345